Around Whitstable

IN OLD PHOTOGRAPHS

Whitstable's very own double act, Fireman Charlie Camburn and son Eric, ready for action. For a number of years in the '30s Eric was the brigade's mascot at shows and carnivals. Both the uniform and brass Trojan-style helmet were specially made.

Around Whitstable

IN OLD PHOTOGRAPHS

Collected by CLIFF COURT

Alan Sutton Publishing Limited
Phoenix Mill · Far Thrupp
Stroud · Gloucestershire

First published 1993

Dedication

To my father Edward, sister Jacqueline and brother Laurence.

British Library Cataloguing
in Publication Data

Court, Cliff
Around Whitstable in Old Photographs
I. Title
942.234

ISBN 0–7509–0398–8

Typeset in 9/10 Sabon.
Typesetting and origination by
Alan Sutton Publishing Limited
Printed in Great Britain by
Redwood Books, Trowbridge.

Contents

Local boatman Mr Edward Court wheels his bike along the prom in around 1948, on the way to where he operated his trip boat during the summer season at Tankerton. This photograph of my father helped generate my interest in looking for others, featuring him down on the beach, a number of years ago. After finding very few I turned to photographs and postcards relating to other aspects of Whitstable and its surrounds, and looking into the history of the area is now one of my interests.

Introduction

Since the 1890s most seaside resorts have been well served by picture postcard publishers. In those early days people would always send one another a brief message on the back of a postcard. However, the photograph used has become even more interesting since it shows scenes of topographical and architectural importance. With the help of former local photographers, you can trace the history of a town, as well as its people, over many years. Photographs take you back to something you remember, or even through to something you never knew. For the last hundred years or so the work of local photographers like P. Barns, S.J. Castle, C.H. Willatt, Filmer, S.M. Goldsmid, S. West, D. West, B. Reeves, Fisk-Moore, H. Silk, and T.H. Staniland has captured scenes for us and left us with an insight of past events.

The town name Whitstable is derived from the ancient British words *whit*, meaning salt, and *stable*, meaning market place. The original township was centred around Church Street and All Saints' church, where old cottages can still be seen. It was not long, however, before the growth of the oyster and other industries led to the building of houses and shops near the coast, and the neighbourhoods of Harbour Street, Sea Street, Middle Wall and Island Wall developed. This is where the boat builders and sailmakers had their yards and it was later regarded as Old Whitstable and the centre of the town's maritime industries.

In the early days Whitstable was always regarded as a working town, where fishing and the harbour were in full swing, unlike those towns further down the coast in Thanet which were regarded as seaside resorts. After the arrival of the railway in 1830, which connected Whitstable to Canterbury, Whitstable became more accessible, but it was not until the 1890s that Whitstable started to become a seaside resort, with the gradual development of Tankerton. The most popular areas were the Slopes and Beach Walk, where bathing machines could be hired and trip boats were available.

Most of the early photographs which I have used in compiling this book are drawn from my own collection. I trust they will provide some idea of what life was like in days gone by, and that you will enjoy this record of Whitstable and some of its people as much as I have enjoyed collecting the material over the years.

SECTION ONE

The Town

Mr William Hayward's bicycle shop at No. 43, Canterbury Road, shown here *c.* 1924. The firm started in 1920. Mr Hayward's partner, a Mr Ashcroft, is pictured here (left) in the doorway with Mr Hayward. Apart from doing all the repairs on bicycles they fitted pram tyres while you waited, and among other accessories sold Ever Ready electric lamps, batteries and wicker cycle baskets. Among makes of bicycle sold were Triumph, Philips, Hercules, BSA, Sturmey Archer (3-speed gear cycles) and, of course, Raleigh. In the '50s mopeds such as Raleigh, Philips and, later on, Jitane, Capitano and Puch came in. After a number of years Mr Hayward and Mr Ashcroft parted company and the latter set up a cycle shop in Cheriton. Mr Hayward's son Geoff came out of the Royal Engineers after the war and started at the shop. His other son, Reg, started in 1949 after coming out of the Royal Air Force, where he was an airframe fitter. Both sons took over on the death of their father in 1950 and continued until 1987, when they retired.

Whitstable Motor & Engineering Works at 14–16 Canterbury Road. Mr W.J. Maflin took over the business in 1929 from Mr T. Rigden, the previous owner. The picture, taken in 1930, shows Mr Maflin on the left, just inside the garage door, with two of his boys, Norman and Ron, on the right and Frank Funnel (driver). Note the early petrol pumps standing on the side of the pavement, close to the road; these were removed when another garage was built further back in the '50s. From the start they ran an old Daimler charabanc as well as an old Ford van. Later they acquired some coaches, which were hired out for outings, schools, etc. Relatives were associated with the Shaftesbury Society in Seasalter, and the coaches were used to take the children on trips and to local carnivals, etc. The business was sold in 1963.

An early scene, looking up Canterbury Road. This postcard from the Kingsway Series is postmarked 1911. Note the couple in the distance with their bikes, walking in the quiet road. One of the old wooden-fronted cottages on the left was the old Railway Hairdressing Salon owned by Mr Rolington.

Mrs Wraight, greengrocer at 49 Canterbury Road, with daughter Ada and surrounded by branches of holly and sacks of chestnuts ready for the festive season, *c.* 1925. The business started from their home in Swanfield Road around 1914, and a hand cart was used for deliveries of produce mostly grown locally. When they moved to the shop a horse and cart was used for deliveries as far away as Herne Bay. The shop normally stayed open until 10 o'clock p.m. and continued trading until 1942.

Customers outside the Golden Lion public house in Belmont Road, Whitstable, prior to their departure for the annual outing in 1934. Regulars include top row: left Fred Horn, fourth Tom Collar, eighth Jack Cage, tenth Fred Hockless, Bona Austin, ? Wanstall, Harry Sandy, Bill Barham (landlord). Bottom row: sixth Harry Cage, Jack Wood, eleventh Mr Cage sen., Lou Christopher.

A crowd gathers in the road underneath the railway bridge in Oxford Street, *c.* 1912, dressed in their smart Sunday clothes and possibly waiting for transport for an outing.

Mr Horace Tustin outside the watchmakers shop, Staddon's, at No. 56 Oxford Street, which he later purchased. After learning the trade in Deal he started work for Staddon's in the early '20s. Later he went away for a few years but on his return in 1932 bought the business. In 1935 he purchased other premises (see p. 17).

A Filmer photograph taken *c.* 1910 of the old Oxford Street Board School, later known as the Old Boy's School. Opened in 1877, it was attended in the years up to the turn of the century by both boys and girls; later it was boys only.

The Oxford Street end of Nelson Road, *c.* 1910. In the years before the turn of the century, after storms and high tides, the sea would occasionally come right up to this point.

F.J. Breaches, Nos 20–22 Oxford Street, one of the earliest garages, was formerly the Old Brewery Tap public house. Engineer Mr Breach converted the building into a garage just before the First World War. This photograph was taken around 1914. Note that bicycles were also sold.

The new premises Mr Tustin had built at No. 21 Oxford Street. Pictured outside are Mrs Joan Tustin and daughter Anne, *c.* 1936. The new shop was larger than the premises at 56 Oxford Street, with double display windows. They also had an assistant that came from the other shop. In 1940 Mr Tustin changed direction, using his skills to make tools for the war effort. In 1947 he opened another jewellery shop at Herne Bay.

A young girl stands neatly dressed with hat and scarf, while a baby sits, well wrapped in a blanket and cosy hat, in a quaint old pram waiting for her picture to be taken in this lovely Filmer photograph, *c.* 1910. St Mary's Parish Hall, Oxford Street is behind. The hall was opened in 1906.

S.T. Gates & Son, ladies outfitters, established in 1932, sold all types of ladies clothing and costumery. The shop was situated at 103–105 High Street. The two women are pictured here in the late '30s. Nancy Grey is on the left. Gates later became Herberts bicycle shop in 1938.

An early Whitstable High Street scene, *c.* 1890, showing F.W. Hawkins, bakers and confectioners, at No. 110. The business was started in the 1880s by Fred Hawkins, pictured here standing in the doorway of his shop; the other person is unknown. They made a whole range of bread, pastries and biscuits which they sold, as well as corn, to customers as far away as Herne Bay, delivering by horse and cart (see p. 157). His two sons later joined him in the business, Frank before the First World War and Alan just after. In 1938 Alan decided to spread his wings and purchased the bakers in Oxford Street. Frank carried on until the fifties.

Children playing in the High Street, alongside the railings of the Congregational church, *c.* 1912. This building dates back to just after the 1800s. Note the girls in their long pinafore dresses, and the boys with caps, old woollen jumpers and knee-length trousers and boots. The boy in the road is wearing a Norfolk jacket and Eton collar.

Men assembled outside the Wall Tavern, Middle Wall for a dart club outing in 1921. Waiting in the road is the transport provided, horse-drawn brakes, with drivers Jack Monk on the left and Fred Dale on the right. Others include Charlie Coleman, Percy Paine, Billy Whorlow, B. Rigden and, landlord at the time, Billy Wise.

Standing outside The Guinea in Island Wall in 1936 is landlady Mrs Minnie Rigden. She ran the pub with husband Fred from 1930 to 1950. Established in around 1860 by Mr William Henry Pettman, at one time this was the only pub in the country of that name. It was used mainly by the locals, especially the fishing and boatyard workers. During the last war the Army were on Emplacement duty across the road in R.J. Perkins' boatyard, from where they used to visit the pub. Before they left for other duties the officers thanked Mrs Rigden for her hospitality.

Henry Daly's grocers shop at No. 87 High Street. Standing outside are some of the family in their long aprons, *c*. 1912. They ran the business from the early 1900s to the '60s.

H.G. Surman's, 61 High Street. In the display for the festive season, *c*. 1913, hang hindquarters of beef and poultry. Pictured wearing his apron is the eldest son, who, on the death of his father, went on to run the shop with his mother.

When this photograph of C.W. Spenceley & Son at 51–53 High Street was taken in August 1930, the shop had just undergone an extension and was now the most up-to-date store of its kind in the district, the shop-front area being almost the size of the Co-op! The work, carried out by Ashby Bros of Regent Street, took six weeks to complete, and was just in time for a summer sale, as the posters indicate. Items included in the sale were two- and three-piece wool suits (usual price 15s 11d, sale price 6s 11d), cashmere jumper suits (5s 11d), and ladies' sleeveless waistcoats in Flannel and velveteen (worth 12s 11d, sale price 1s 11d). All cotton frocks were to be cleared for 1s 6d; tweed skirts 1s 6d; leather gloves absurd prices 1s a pair; a few ladies' macs to be cleared at 5s each. Blankets (heavy, all wool) 88 in by 88 in were 10s 11d each. A pair of white sheets 70 in by 100 in was 5s 11d. The business was established in 1890 by Chapman Spenceley and his son Wilfred ran the shop until 1951, when Ricemans took over.

High Street, *c.* 1912, with two boys in the middle of the street, one sitting in a hand cart and both looking out for the photographer. Shops to the right of the picture include the Model Dairy, the Worlds Store and the old post office built just after the turn of the century.

High Street, 1920s, taken in the warmer months. Shops on the left include Scott and Son, dyers, A.E. Cooke and, with canopy, West & Son, photographers. Across the street a lorry is unloaded outside Surman's the butchers.

A deserted, snow-laden High Street, photographed by the late D. West in January 1940. The time is 12.20 p.m. according to the clock above Surman's shop. In the distance is the imposing shape of the Old Argosy Cinema, now a supermarket.

The Bear & Key, *c.* 1925, showing the then owner, Mr Fred Appleton, standing alongside one of the horses which was kept in stables behind the pub. Sitting on the horse is Mr Rippingall, the riding-master. The Daimler parked at the front entrance was owned by Mr Appleton; at the wheel sits Mr Sidney Earthy. Mr Burt Ashby's old Ford taxi is behind. Mr Appleton had the Bear & Key for some forty years after starting in 1919. The pub dates back some 400 years.

Tom Britcher, wearing hat and apron, stands alongside his fruit, veg and shellfish stall on the corner of Sea Street, across from the Horsebridge, *c.* 1958. With him outside the Prince Albert is landlord Horace Cullen. A stallholder for many years, Tom started by selling seafood from a barrow. Some of the prices are: whelks 2s 6d a pint, tomatoes 1s 8d, grapes 2s per pound.

This view, taken around 1911 by B. Reeves, photographer of Whitstable, shows in the distance the tall sailing masts of the vessels in the Harbour. In the foreground the old shop, John Uptons (stationer), is at 59 Harbour Street, on the corner of Sydenham Street.

Looking down from Ludgate Hill into Harbour Street. The couple with an elegant pram manoeuvre across to the centre of the road, something that would be quite dangerous today. To the left of the picture is the Railway Tavern, Flint and Co. Ales, which today is the Punch Tavern, and to the right is the unusual wedge-shaped building owned by F. Goldfinch and built about 1905.

Tower Parade. Children in their summer outfits can be seen with their parents beside a horse-drawn cab rank by a piece of ground used as a shrub garden that jutted out into the road. The Jubilee Memorial fountain was situated here. In the distance is the Castle Gate, entrance to the Tower Gardens. Visitors to the beach would pass here from the 'Crab and Winkle Line' station just up the road.

Mr Charles Coleman standing in the doorway of Tower Stores, his grocery shop on the corner of Tankerton Terrace and Northwood Road, *c.* 1902. A lot of the produce that was sold can be seen neatly displayed in the large windows, along with posters and adverts for jam, teas, butters, bacon, etc. He took over the shop, which was already a grocers, in 1900 and carried on the business until 1916. He had an assistant, and provisions and paraffin were delivered to customers in Tankerton and Northwood Road by hand cart. His son Harold, who was born at the shop, used to go along with the delivery cart. In the early days provisions came down from London by barge, were unloaded at the Horsebridge by the Whitstable Hoy Company, then distributed to the shops. During the First World War some soldiers from the 8th Irish Regiment were billeted at the shop.

SECTION TWO

Disasters

The fate of the Avro Anson aircraft after ditching into the sea off Whitstable during an experimental flight from Manston in 1936. Local boatmen were quickly on the scene to find the pilot unhurt. A line was attached to the plane, which was able to float. The tail end is seen here being towed to the beach at the Horsebridge where the RAF arranged for its removal back to base.

Loss of the 141 Seaplane off Whitstable on 28 July 1914. The pilot of the plane was a captain R.J. Bone, who was rescued by local boats and was lucky to survive. This was his only recorded crash. He joined the Navy in 1904 and served in submarines, afterwards joining the Royal Naval Air Service in 1913. Later he flew in the anti-Zeppelin patrols. In 1916 he won the DSO for forcing down a German seaplane which was bombing Margate. After a distinguished career abroad, covering four continents and thirty-four years flying, he became Commanding Officer RAF Pembroke Dock.

A barge lashed by heavy seas against the beach at Whitstable, after breaking its moorings and being driven ashore, *c.* 1925. In those days there were many more boats laying off, or trading these shores, so during heavy storms it was inevitable that some would end up this way.

A crowd gathers in around 1930, as an oyster yawl lies beached on the west side of the Harbour after dragging its anchor in a gale. Registered F7, the *Clyde* was built in Essex in 1919, dimensions 40.57 x 11.6 x 5.2; her owners were John Warner and J. Marshall, and Master J. Harman.

After the storm of 4 December 1920. People gather among the wreckage strewn over the Reeves Beach area. In the distance lies an old oyster yawl which, after dragging its anchor, has been driven ashore.

An early occurrence of the Whitstable floods. This photograph shows Westgate Terrace, Wave Crest, in 1897, with the sea water rising quickly across the flats, or saltings as they were known, which later became the Seasalter golf course.

One of the earliest photographs in the book, an illustration of the frozen seas off Whitstable, looking west from the Harbour area, and showing yawls and barges surrounded by packs of ice. (From a Filmer photograph of 1895.)

Off the Horsebridge, Whitstable, January 1940. Charlie is down by the Harbour 'winkling'; can you pick him out?

Imprisoned in ice off Whitstable, February 1929. This was to be one of the worst years for frozen seas, which lasted for many weeks. Five men employed on the watch boats who set off back to shore for provisions were trapped for nine hours. This shows the rescue of two of the oyster smack watchmen who got into difficulty. After setting out at 6 a.m., three men, B.M. Stroud, E.J. Rowden and H. Goodburn (all employed by Seasalter & Ham Oyster Fishery Co.) in one boat, and a father and son in another, were unable to negotiate the masses of ice which barred their progress. From 7.30 they battled for three hours, after which time a rescue party made up of John Warner, Charles Camburn, Walter Stroud, W.H. Care, F. Ashby and Robert Dale started off in a skiff, hacking a path through the ice, leaving a rope trailing back to shore to pull them to safety. The three men had by now boarded the *Emma* for shelter from the cold. The rescue party joined them and they made headway to the yawl *Bluebell*, reaching her by 1 p.m. An attempt was made by the crowds gathered on the beach to pull the rope and boat back, but to no avail. The rope had frozen in the ice and finally snapped. The men, now exhausted, made for the motor boat *Speedwell*, and the engine was thawed and started, giving the boat enough power to cut through the ice to Messrs Waters senior and junior (employed by George Tabor Ltd). All finally reached shore by 5 p.m.

A frozen Harbour in February 1956, looking in from the west side. Most of the smaller craft are frozen solid in the ice. Moored alongside a cargo vessel, on the east quay, is the fishing boat *Romulus*, owned by the Leggatts. Some years would prove to be worse than others, and the fishermen would bear the brunt of the severe weather, sometimes not being able to work for weeks.

Left high and dry. The Russian cargo ship *Aura* went aground on Tankerton's infamous 'Street' shingle bar, *en route* for Whitstable Harbour, *c.* 1920. The *Aura* was an iron-hulled vessel of 134 gross tons, built by Hjalmare Dockha. She was 99.8 ft in length, with a 17.8 ft beam. She may have come in towards the Harbour on a tight bearing or she was blown off course. It is quite possible she was refloated on the next high tide.

Can you spot the green, and where do you 'tee off' from? The devastating floods of 1953 cut off the clubhouse at Seasalter golf links.

A row of pumps from the Kent Fire Brigade stretch across Waterloo Road, Whitstable, during the flood disaster of February 1953. At one point the water had risen to a level of about 5 ft along here. The firemen worked hard for many hours to reduce the level, the water being pumped back into the sea.

A deluge of rain fell in August 1939, just before the outbreak of war. In no time at all it had risen to a depth of around 5 inches. At that moment D. West stepped outside his shop in the High Street and took these pictures.

The Assembly Rooms have been blasted, part of the side wall has collapsed and the roof has fallen in, the result of a bombing raid in the Second World War. To the side, the Painted Lady Café has received damage, but the Fire Station, with its air raid siren above, remains intact. The firemen, pictured from second left, are Wesley Poole, Jack Lawson, Ted Savage, Vic Rigden and Alf Prescott. Prior to the raid, at approximately 7.10 a.m. on 3 August 1941, Alf Prescott was outside the station having a cup of tea with colleagues when enemy planes came over. Firemen rushed for cover as one bomb exploded. The blast knocked the cup Alf was holding away, leaving him with just the handle!

Inspecting the damage after the fire at the Rosary, a bungalow next to the Rose in Bloom pub in Joy Lane, in the late '20s; Firemen Tom Rigden (on the left) and Punch Olive are both wearing the old style helmets of the time. The building, once used by coast guards, was constructed of timber. It was severely damaged and had to be rebuilt; it later became Tree Tops Guest House.

Damping down at Seaths timber yard, Cromwell Road, 1932. This was just one of a series of fires that occurred that year, the work of an arsonist. Not a week went by without a serious outbreak, apparently on Wednesday evenings. It was reported at the time that many business people received warnings. Some of the other buildings affected by fire were another timber yard, a boatyard, a furnishing store, Spenceleys, an arcade, a printers, a boarding house and a fruiterers store.

Members of the Whitstable Fire Brigade gather outside Offredi's Restaurant, 29 High Street, soon after the fire which destroyed most of the interior, *c.* 1916. The scorched upstairs window can clearly be seen. In the window on the ground floor an advert reads 'Pot of Tea 5d, Ices 2d, 4d & 6d'.

The most spectacular blaze seen in Whitstable since the famous Wednesday night fires of the early '30s attracted a huge crowd one early Saturday afternoon on 3 July 1937, when a three-storey building, an annexe to St Mary's High School, Northwood Road, was almost completely destroyed within half an hour of the alarm being raised. At the scene was Chief Fire Officer G.W. Fisher. The cause of the outbreak was a mystery, one theory being that the intense heat of the sun reflected through a piece of glass onto some combustible material may have started the blaze. However, it is interesting to recall that during the series of Wednesday night fires a warning was received threatening that the school would be 'Fired'!

Aftermath of a fire at the Old Steam Packet pub, October 1913. The pub, mostly of timber construction, stood just in front of the Harbour. It was rebuilt after the devastating blaze. Standing in front of the ruins on the right are two firemen, a policeman and a man in a boater hat (could this be the landlord?).

Being retrieved from a ditch on the old road between Herne Bay and Swalecliffe is an old Aveling Porter road roller (reg KK1227) built at Rochester in 1902. It was owned by the Wingham Engineering Co. Ltd, whose Office Manager can be seen wearing a light grey overcoat and trilby hat. The accident occurred in the early '20s, the 10-ton roller going over on its side. The steam roller was eventually pulled clear by the two steam ploughing engines, owned by local farmer Mr Pout of Kite Farm, which were working nearby.

Adults and children outside the home of Mrs Wall at 73 Canterbury Road after a gas explosion on 19 June 1909 blew the front of the house out. Earlier Mrs Wall had contacted the gas company, as insufficient gas was coming through her stove. Two employees arrived that morning and pumped out the meter, but Mr Wyver, one employee, struck a match near the gas stove! An explosion of surprising violence blew out the front windows and door, particles of which were blown through the windows of houses opposite. Mrs Wall and her daughter were in the house at the time though miraculously neither they nor the gas employees sustained injury when Mrs Wall's 'walls' collapsed around her. Adjoining houses suffered considerable damage, the party walls being forced outwards. Total damage was probably four or five hundred pounds.

SECTION THREE

The Seaside

An early bathing scene at Seasalter, from before the First World War. The message on the back of the postcard reads, 'If you happen to have bathing suits they will come in handy, as you will see by the card that we have a good time in the briny.' Note the costumes of the time, the men in their pyjama-like clothing and the ladies with their dressing-gown-type costumes. The lady sitting in the clinker built rowing boat is shaded by her parasol, probably to keep her complexion 'nice 'n' white'.

A delightful scene showing children sitting on the pebbles at West Beach, *c.* 1910, the girls in their Sunday best dresses and bonnets, the boys in Norfolk jackets and Eton collars. Just behind on the shoreline stands the Old Neptune public house; beyond that a brig sits high up on a slipway, while in the distance ships can be seen in the Harbour area.

Marine Terrace, West Beach, quite an early scene from a Bell Series postcard postmarked July 1913. Note the beach is all open at this point. Women and children wearing long dresses and bonnets are relaxing on a bench.

Children amuse themselves at the water's edge at Reeves Beach, 1928. Out in the bay the oyster fleet rests in a calm sea.

Whitstable's version of the Loch Ness monster, photographed here on the long beach by S. West, *c.* 1925. In the early part of the twentieth century whales were often stranded in shallow waters, most not being refloated in time. If the old fishermen could not get them back into the water they would sell the carcasses for oil or manure. Also pictured here between the Wood brothers, third and fifth from right, is the well-known photographer, the late Douglas West.

The crowd gathers for the annual Regatta, held at this time (1907) off the Beach Walk area. To complete their Edwardian summer outfits, most men, women and children are wearing hats of all different shapes and styles. In the centre foreground of the photograph, on the left of the lady with the umbrella, a young Wallace Harvey, later the well-known local historian, can be seen sitting in his pram.

A group of Guides at Beach Walk, Tankerton, 1937. The circular shaped apparatus to the right was known as 'Bubbles'. Compressed air was blown through the middle, causing balls to rise up and down, the object being to catch at least three balls with a small hand-held net to win a prize.

A familiar site on the beach at Tankerton, remembered by visitors and locals alike, these old swing-boats were erected in the 1890s. Children are happily riding on them in around 1920. The building with the balcony behind is the Beulah Hotel in Beach Road. The swings were dismantled after the 1953 storm.

On the beach at Tankerton, *c.* 1911, showing the Hotel Beulah, proprietor Mrs A. Bockmaster. To the right is the Marine Café, owned by V. Offredi. In later years the Beulah was extended and became known as The Continental, the bar occupying the original Marine Café building. More recently the bar was known as the Harbour Lights. On the beach in front of the building can be seen the box-type benches which the boatmen used to store their oars, etc.

Schoolchildren aboard the *Moss Rose* at Tankerton in June 1922. This sailing craft was the first pleasure boat of that name owned by the Waters Bros. This particular trip was across to the Isle of Sheppey.

All aboard for a trip on the *Monarch* pleasure boat at Tankerton, *c.* 1955. Clinker built and 24 ft long she was owned at one time by the Waters. *Moss Rose II* can be seen behind. One could take a trip around the bay or along the coast towards Herne Bay; larger craft went over to Sheppey.

Ready for a trip over to Sheppey, pleasure boat the *Water Lily* waits at Tankerton Beach in July 1926. She was a larger vessel than the *Monarch* of some 45 ft in length. Around this time the return fare to Sheppey was 2s. Children went half price. Another trip would be around the oyster beds for 1s, children 6d.

The shingle bank at Tankerton known as the 'Street'. When uncovered it stretches out for a mile or so, and families may walk here and explore the sea life. Local boatmen manoeuvred round to the west side of this natural barrier just before the tide ebbed, to where the water was deeper, so they could carry on with their boat trips. The *Moss Rose* pleasure boat can be seen on this side.

Boating at Tankerton, on an old postcard dated 1912. This lovely scene shows trippers disembarking from one of the many small craft which used to work the beaches along Tankerton. The women can be seen wearing the attractive long dresses of the period and wide brimmed hats to keep the sun off their faces.

Pleasure boats were a familiar site at Tankerton, where they could be seen plying for trade off the beaches from the 1890s right through to the 1950s. Here we see an early boatman (*c.* 1900) as he sits relaxing against his lovely old clinker built boat, this one capable of carrying three to four passengers for about 3d or 6d a head. The boat's name, usually of a loved one, was carved in the shaped seat back at the stern. Some of the families involved included the Udens, Kelsleys, Courts, Warners and Waters. Between them they would have a numerous array of craft including sailing ketches, large open motor launches, rowing boats, canoes and pedaloes. The smaller vessels were normally hired out. When on the water one could also be serenaded with music from the old bandstand.

Monday morning washday on Tankerton Beach, *c.* 1910. This working scene shows the men who were involved with the hire of bathing machines and costumes, which were washed after use and hung on the line you can see. The man in charge of this operation was Mr Sampson, who stands on the left wearing a white cap.

Tankerton from the sea, an advertisement used to help publicize the area and extol its health-giving virtues in the '30s.

The Slopes are swarming with people for the annual Regatta, held at Tankerton since the 1790s. (From a photograph by B. Reeves, 1907.)

An array of boats gather for the annual Regatta off Tankerton before the First World War. Apart from the war years, it has been held annually since the 1790s, and swimming events, rowing, sailing, and soot and flour matches between smacks and fishing vessels have taken place. On one occasion in the '30s pilot Captain King flew over in his Dessouter from Swalecliffe, diving over the boats and dropping flour bombs. One of the favourite events was of course the slippery pole.

All aboard for the Regatta. An outing on the whelk boat *Three Brothers* for a trip around to Tankerton in 1922, to join the fun and festivities, was arranged for the Court families by my grandfather Fred and uncle Albert Court. Those on deck include my father Edward, uncles Bernard and Albert, Aunts Win, Dorothy and Kate, cousin Dolly, Laurence Horseman and Albert Doughty.

Members of the committee on their boat off Tankerton during the Regatta in the '30s. The old gentleman on the far right is Biscuits Goldfinch, a well-known Whitstable native. Heading a number of committees, his work and interests were many, and mostly for the good of the town. Sitting next to him is Mr George Taylor.

F.S. Gann's motor cruiser, the *Moggee*, seen here off Tankerton flying the flags for the Regatta, *c.* 1937. Built by R.J. Perkins in the '20s, she was 40 ft long and had Morris twin engines under the wheel house. On deck at midships, wearing a cap, is Mr Gann; seated behind him is Mrs Gann. Also on board are other members of the family, while at the wheel is Mr George Pattenden sen. Mr Gann was a builder in the town as well as a keen fisherman who took part in a lot of competitions.

The fishing boat *Cortina* F27, owned by the Leggatts, lays off the beach at Tankerton for a '50s Regatta. On board having fun are left Joan Leggatt, middle George Leggatt and far right Alf Leggatt. Taking place on deck is the 'crossing the Equator' type ceremony. Alf was always involved one way or another with Regattas and carnivals throughout the '50s.

For many years the St John Ambulance Brigade had a medical hut, erected in the '30s, on the Promenade at Tankerton right opposite the shingle bank known as the 'Street'. The staff used to man the station mainly at weekends during the summer months. This particular picture was taken by Holiday Snaps of Margate around 1950 and shows Nurse Mabel Godley, ex-Fireman Punch Olive and Nurse Dorothy Jones.

Romany Cottage, Marine Parade. Soldiers stand by the fence with nurses behind during the First World War. The building was used as a convalescent home for the wounded, especially those affected by gas, the sea air helping their lungs. The cottage is still there and is one of the oldest along Marine Parade.

A popular venue on the Slopes at Tankerton was the old bandstand, situated on the east side of the 'Street' shingle bank among the bathing huts. The Whitstable Town Band and others used to play here. Erected in the early 1900s it used to give a great deal of pleasure to locals and holiday-makers right up to the '40s, when it was pulled down.

Seen not long after being erected in 1908, this shelter stands in its original position, opposite St Anne's Road on Marine Parade. Behind on the left is the old 'Pavilion' building, the Marine Hotel. The shelter was later moved to another position along the Slopes, adjacent to Graystone Road.

This postcard appeared in the local newspaper around ten years ago with the heading 'A part of the town that hasn't altered'. The card dates from 1931 and was sent by John Markham, a regular visitor here, to his father in Coulsdon in Surrey. The newspaper article went on to say that the area around the 'Marine' has hardly changed, and that if you look closely at the pavement several large cracks can be seen. Some would argue these haven't changed much over the years! The cost of sending this card was one old penny and the chances are it arrived next day!

What a nice composition these children make in this early photograph taken by Faversham photographer W. Hargrave at Tankerton Slopes in 1908.

Café Royal Hotel, Marine Parade, Tankerton (proprietor Mr J.W. Reeves, est. *c.* 1930), on a D. West postcard of 1948. This restaurant and hotel had previously been a café. The building on the right with the pitched roof is part of the original. Evening dances were held here during the summer. The vehicle standing out front is an old Crossley owned at one time by S. West, photographer.

Aerial view showing Priest & Sow Corner, *c.* 1930s. Along the seafront at this point was a long line of beach huts (now no longer there) and just off the shore was the old wooden diving platform that used to shake. A few open spaces can be seen off the main road and Cliff Stores can also be seen near the corner. To the left of the picture and out of sight there used to be a strip of land used for an emergency runway.

Cliff Stores, situated on the seafront at Priest & Sow Corner. This was a busy little shop then, as it is now, for both locals and visitors. One could get most provisions here and teas were served in the back. Within the last few years the building has been totally modernized and enlarged. This picture was taken in around 1936.

Bathing Belles at Tankerton, 1935. These girls were featured in the *Whitstable Guide* as part of a publicity campaign to promote the town. The girls, all local, were chosen from shops in the High Street where they worked. From left to right are Peggy Luckhurst, Betty Halls, Vera Stroud, Nora Richards and Ruth Oliver. Who wouldn't be a shrimp?

SECTION FOUR

Transport

Mr Wall Smith, baker, at the bottom of Borstal Hill, *c.* 1906. Smith the bakers was first established in 1906 at 72 High Street, previously the site of Reeves bakery, and later moved to 69 High Street, on the corner of Gladstone Road. Smith's was very obliging at Christmas time, allowing customers to use the ovens for the baking of their own turkeys, puddings and cakes. The late Mr John Smith took over the business on the death of his father.

Nuttens Coal Merchants, 1 Victoria Street, *c.* 1916. The young man holding the reins is believed to be Ted Nutten, who had a brother Bob. They distributed foodstuffs from the railway station to the local shops, and carried passengers' luggage, as well as working at the Horsebridge using what was known as a tip cart to load and carry oysters to the stores.

Soft fruit (cherries) in wicker baskets being unloaded from an old farm cart on to railway trucks waiting on the main line. To the left of the cart can be seen an old Model T Ford, *c.* 1920s.

Two of E.J. Pout's steam ploughing engines on the farm at Swalecliffe in the mid-'30s, both built in Leeds around 1916 with F7 Fowler compound engines. One is named *General French*, No. KE3134, and the other *Lord Kitchener*, No. KE3135.

Sitting on an early NSU German-built vee-twin cylinder motorcycle at the end of the alleyway along by the railway embankment in Oxford Street around 1910 is Mr Cecil Wheeler, who owned a bicycle shop at No. 73. He established the business in 1906 and continued trading until 1919. Later he had a sweet shop at No. 1 Oxford Street. Mr Wheeler was also one of the first people in the town to have a motor car.

An outing in the country. Mr Cecil Wheeler, his wife Maud and son Roy aboard an old Bradbury combination, *c.* 1913. The mother and son, cosily wrapped with a leg covering, are sitting in the side-car made of wicker. The motorcycle had a single cyclinder engine with two-speed gears.

Len Rigden with his new trades bike in the back yard of No. 23 High Street, *c.* 1925. His father Tom was a seed and corn merchant. Len delivered goods all over the town and to Tankerton where, at times, it was hard going, several roads being unmade in those days.

The Model T Ford of Tom Rigden, corn merchant, trading from 23 High Street. This picture was taken in the back yard in the '20s. Sitting in the vehicle is Maud Rigden, standing is Len Rigden, and lying on the ground is 'Bubbles' Boulting.

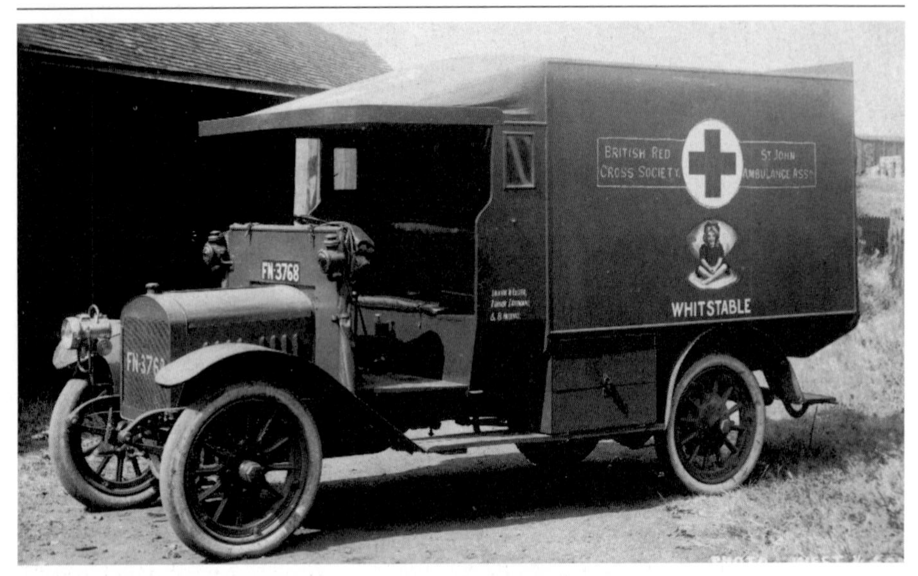

The old Whitstable ambulance, *c.* 1920. This Model T Ford was jointly owned by the British Red Cross Society and the St John Ambulance Association, and was one of the earliest in the town. Printed on the side of the vehicle was 'Load not to exceed 1 driver, 1 attendant, 8 patients'. The tyres were tubed and it had paraffin oil side and rear lamps; the large lamp on the front was an acetylene type.

Pub outing aboard an old Daimler charabanc, Sunday 6 July 1924. These outings were quite an event and the local men used to look forward to them in the summer. The journeys would take them to various locations in the country and a particular favourite was to Rye via Tenterden. Pictured are the driver Tom Rigden, who owned the vehicle, Harold Biggs, sitting next to him on the left, and behind and between the two is Bill London. Third left from the front is Robert Court (fishmonger) and Bill Burden is far right at the front.

Mr Standen (with top hat) alongside his milkmen in this carnival picture taken in Cromwell Road, *c.* 1934. From the left: Boxer Fuller, standing, Mr Garlinge, sitting, Mr Standen's grandson, Mr Standen and the late Harold Butcher. The delivery vans were belt-driven Trojans. The slogan on the front vehicle reads, 'Don't hope for the best, let us bring it to you.' The company was established in the '20s by Mr S. Standen, with dairies at Clapham Hill and Chestfield. The depot was on the corner of Nelson Road and Cornwallis Circle. At that time it was a 5 a.m. start and you worked until 5 p.m., seven days a week, with just four days off per year. The price of milk was about 3d per pint.

A small fleet of vehicles belonging to Arthur Collar, the ironmongers and builders merchants of 35 High Street, parked along Regent Street in 1935. Drivers include Vic Whorlow, on the motorcycle combination, Walter Scott, standing by his 30 cwt Morris, and, along from him, Stan Rigden with his 1 ton Morris. The last vehicle, a Model T Ford, was one of the company's first; it had previously been used as an ambulance. On one evening during the last war a parachute bomb demolished part of this area, destroying the garage seen in the photograph and, among other buildings, a fish and chip shop in Victoria Street opposite where a girl and a young soldier were killed.

T.G. Browning and Sons was established in 1860 and traded until 1961. The company, started in the days of horse and carts, carried out removals, coal deliveries and haulage business for people in the Whitstable area. It had two depots, one at the Horsebridge and another in Canterbury Road, and its vehicles were a familiar site in the town. The lorry pictured in Saddleton Road in 1925 is a Palladium with solid tyres. It had a propshaft handbrake which shuddered when applied. The vehicle originally came from France in 1919. In the driving seat is Charlie Waters. This particular model had a detachable container which could be transferred on to a flat-bed railway truck in the goods yard at the Oxford Street station.

Firemen's mascots. Whitstable's Eric Camburn (standing) and Faversham's Jackie Beamont (seated) are wearing official uniforms and on board their little engine, complete with bell, hoses and ladder, at a local show. Eric was the son of Whitstable fireman Charlie Camburn.

The Merryweather fire engine, Whitstable's first motorized appliance, known as the 'Native', seen here in a carnival procession in 1930. The firemen are all wearing brass helmets. Up front in pride of place is mascot Eric Camburn and with him, driver Tom Rigden; others include Charlie Camburn, Punch Olive, Edgerton Moyes and Cracker Smith. When the new engine was purchased Tom Rigden went to Croydon to collect it.

Tom Wesson, passing in search of customers, in an old taxi complete with advertising posters and a board on the roof with the words 'Stop Me and Fly One'. He would bring people back to Swalecliffe Airfield, part of the old Kite Farm, where Captain King would be waiting in his three-seater Desoutter monoplane to take them for a wonderful flight around the bay for five shillings.

Sir Alan Cobham's DH Giant Moth *Youth of Britain* sits on a landing field at Kite Farm, Swalecliffe, owned by Mr George Pout in 1929. When he arrived he was introduced to well-known local people, the purpose of his visit being to try and establish an official airfield at the site. The plane had a 500 hp Armstrong Siddeley Jaguar engine.

The assembly line of George Fitt Motors, Tankerton, *c.* 1946. The men busy here assembling the early propelled invalid cars include, from third left: ? Simpson, Peter Rivers and George Silk. The building in use had been part of the old Troc Cinema. These cars, designed at Fitt's by Mr C.J. Turner, were propelled by means of a lever which operated a gear to turn the wheels; steering was by use of a handle. After inspecting the early models, Ministry of Health officials later awarded Fitt's the contract. Every so often inspectors would arrive and test them. During the war years Fitt's did machine work for Short Bros and converted large cars to ambulances.

One of the many invalid cars that were designed and built at George Fitt Motors, Tankerton, this particular model was especially made to measure for this man, a resident at Morris House, Westgate. The picture was taken in Tankerton in the early '50s. The vehicle had a single cylinder 197 cc Villiers engine with a self starter and was capable of 30 m.p.h. These open type cars were produced until the late '50s. A wheelchair was attached to the side of this model, which could be assembled ready for use.

The Chestfield Filling Station, Thanet Way, *c.* 1948. Owned by George Fitt Motors, this art deco design of the 1930s was quite noticeable. In the '70s another station was built around this older one, which was eventually demolished.

Four firemen from the AFS unit stand on the back of a Star Minerals Bedford truck, with a Dennis 500-gallons-a-minute water pump in tow, parked along Cromwell Road, outside Seaths timber yard, *c.* 1940. In the background is A. Rye & Sons, Furnishers, now the *Whitstable Times* building. Pictured from left: Harold Butcher, George Ford, Bill Bright, ? Whorlow.

AFS firemen with a George Fitt Motors fire tender in 1940. The vehicle with pump in tow is a large old American Stutz. The location is outside A. Rye & Sons, Furnishers. Those known are, third from left, Bill Potter, with Vic Rigden on his left.

Ready to climb aboard one of Grey's lorries, an Austin 5 tonner loaded with fruit boxes, is Mr E. Grey, *c.* 1950. Mr Albert Grey used to buy up the fruit grown in local orchards, and deliver it to Wales. In fact, Mr Grey dealt in anything, with anybody. He also kept horses in a field opposite the Four Horseshoes pub on Borstal Hill.

Mr Bill Gibbens next to one of Cages coal lorries, on the old railbank above Belmont Road, *c.* 1956. Bill and Fred Hinkley, who used to drive the vehicle, an Austin, worked together delivering coal.

A rare postcard entitled 'Bridges for All', adapted from one of local artist Dan Sherrin's works which showed various ways of crossing the Swale, between the mainland and the Isle of Sheppey. Sherrin (1869–1940) has even included himself fishing from the river bank, wearing his loud check suit! (Is his thumb print the seal of approval?) A prolific artist, Sherrin worked mainly in oils, producing landscapes, seascapes and still lifes. He would on occasions settle his bills to traders with paintings.

SECTION FIVE

Maritime

Preparing to slip into the water at Perkins Yard, Island Wall, is the barquentine *Speedwell* in 1913. Built in 1878 at Kingston-on-Spey, Scotland, she weighed 198 tons and was owned by Abbey Andersons. One of her early masters was Daniel Court. The bottom picture shows her fully afloat after re-launching, with flags flying aft.

On board a brigantine believed to be the *Thames, c.* 1900. Huge masts with rigging attached tower above the young seaman on this old square rigged trader. Built in 1875 by Marshall at Plymouth, of 176 registered tons, and owned by the Whitstable Shipping Company, one of her masters was local man Capt. Ericson. Before the turn of the century boys went to sea at 14 with a six or seven year apprenticeship ahead of them. Although conditions were gradually improving, life on board was still fairly hard, endless hours being worked, especially at sea during rough weather. Cargoes other than coal included chalk, on return to Sunderland, or imports of timber.

The *Hilda*, a barquentine, on the East Quay of Whitstable Harbour, *c.* 1914. On the quayside below the old chimney stands an early mechanically-operated crane and, to the side, a row of coal trucks. The *Hilda*, owned by the Whitstable Shipping Company, was built in 1879 by Pickard at Appledore, Devon reg. no. 223, weight 160 tons, length 116 ft 5 in, beam 24 ft 9 in, masters T.S. Sweetman of Gladstone Road, J. Sinclair, ? Thundow. For many years this vessel was a familiar sight here, carrying cargoes of coal and chalk. Other journeys would include trips across the Atlantic for sugar, spices and wheat. She was sunk in a collision off Nova Scotia on 9 December 1930.

Opposite:
On board the re-rigged barquentine *Hilda*, moored in the Harbour, *c.* 1914. Two crew members prepare to winch out their cargo, which was usually loaded into large wicker baskets. Among the cargoes discharged were coal, chalk, ballast and stone.

Men working on the Harbour Quay, unloading coal from colliers, 1919. This was done in two stages. First men would shovel the coal from the hold into large baskets. When loaded a rope with a hook was attached, which would then be hauled up by men on deck climbing a wooden ladder and jumping to a lower level. This was sufficient to raise the basket up on deck next to the hatch. Then an upper hook was attached and two men on the quayside would mount a wooden structure known as the jumping horse. By taking in the slack rope then jumping backwards the basket would be raised off the hatch and swung round on to the railway trucks. The last time this method was used was in around 1928. It was very hard work and all done for a pittance.

A Harbour scene, showing old colliery boats, on a postcard dated 1910. The closest ship can be identified as the *Raven*, a brigantine built in 1873 by James Duncan at Bay Fortune Bridge, Prince Edward Island, reg. no. 177, length 106 ft, beam 24 ft, weight 160 tons approximately. Among the owners were J.G. Gann (1915), T.R. Dadd, George Gann and Pout; the masters were E. Blaxland and H.W. Beesley. Although mostly engaged in transporting coal from Sunderland, among the other cargo imported was stone and timber. The *Raven* was later sold to a London company.

A smart looking postman visits the Harbour during his deliveries, *c.* 1913. Old colliers can be seen moored alongside the west and east quays.

Looking east along West Beach, this early shipyard scene is from a Filmer photograph of *c.* 1906. High up on a slipway sits the *Hildred*, a brigantine being repaired by one of the shipyards of the time. Built at Prince Edward Island in 1878, 115 ft long, and 224 tons, she was owned by the Whitstable Shipping Company at one time. Many of these ships were engaged in transporting coal from Sunderland. Beached high up in front of the brigantine is an old barge, and in the foreground three boys are amusing themselves posing for their picture.

Oyster fishermen about to row out to their smacks, which were moored offshore in the bay, *c.* 1930. When they were dredging, these small boats (skiffs) would be towed behind. There were normally four fishermen to a smack.

The crew of the smack 59F *Ada Maria* hauling in their dredges. The picture was taken at a busy time *c.* 1930.

Smacksmen hauling their catch of oysters over the rail, photographed before the First World War. They will soon set about culling the oysters, throwing away what they don't require.

Landing the oysters at the Horsebridge, *c.* 1907. Men are unloading from a small boat (skiff), while a horse with a two-wheeled cart waits to be loaded. The produce will then be taken to the Oyster Fishery Co. Stores to be sorted.

Having arrived at the store, the oysters are sorted and graded before being packed for market, most going to London.

Whitstable fishermen on board an oyster smack, *c.* 1930. From the left are George Gibbs, Nat Camburn, Percy Gibbens and Mr J. Care. The men, wearing the traditional clothing of Guernsey and cheesecutter caps, needed strong hands and arms to haul in their catches.

Out in the whelk boat, the *Three Brothers*, in 1939. Getting ready to shoot the whelkpots over the side are my uncles, brothers Harry Court (left) and Albert; Fred, my grandfather, the eldest, (all were Whitstable natives) would be back at the sheds preparing the coppers. The pots they used had heavy iron bases, which had a series of holes in them, and were about 13 inches in diameter. Coming up from the base were iron rods curved in the shape of a beehive, and attached to the top was a ring opening of 8 inches. The sides of the pots were finished off with several turns of rope, woven between the rods all the way round. The pots were about 1 ft in height. They were hung by a long shank (rope), with about twenty pots on each shank and a marker buoy attached. They were lifted and re-baited everyday; the best bait was usually skate, offal or herring. Most boats would carry between 100 and 120 pots.

Whelkers Harry Court (left) and Albert shooting a pot over the side of *Three Brothers II* (F89) in 1951. The boat was made locally in 1949, length 24 ft, beam 8 ft 6 in. Having slipped out of harbour in the early hours, areas worked were either off Reculver or on to Birchington in one direction, or over to Sheppey and on to Sheerness. The whelkpots were placed on suitable ground, such as the yellow slippery clay of the Kentish flats, which contains red worms on which the whelks feed. The depth of seabed averaged six fathoms. Hermit crabs could play havoc by going after the same bait as the whelks; eating crabs and lobsters were also found in the pots. Whelks can usually be caught all the year round, unless the water is too warm or too cold in which case the whelks will not crawl.

Landing the whelks on the east quay of the Harbour, 1951. Harry Court is clearing up while Albert Court stands by the wash-sized net bags of whelks, which are ready to be hauled ashore and taken to the old sheds situated behind the Engine House chimney, where they would be boiled in the coppers.

Three Brothers II, pictured on the west side of Tankerton shingle bank (the 'Street') in 1951. Harry Court starts to burn off the old tar from the keel; afterwards fresh tar would be applied in a process known as blacking.

Harry and Albert Court bagging up the whelks outside the sheds in 1922. Once cooked in their net bags, the whelks are dried and any empty shells are culled out. They are then bagged ready for market, priced by the five-gallon-load of whelks in their shells which was called a wash. Whelking by local men was taking place from these shores prior to the 1890s, but it really got under way when the whelkpot came into being, after the arrival of families from Sheringham in Norfolk. About a dozen families came south in boats loaded with their possessions, and many settled in Whitstable, to make their living from whelking.

R.J. Perkins & Sons was one of the busiest boatyards in the town, established around 1918 in Island Wall. As well as building boats for local people it did work for the Admiralty. Among the types of vessels built were Admiral Barges (double skinned), 52 ft steam pinnaces (carvel built), 27 ft whalers (clinker built), 52 ft Customs boats, pilot boats, 45 ft Liberty boats (double skins), open for carrying passengers and harbour work. They also converted Naval cutters to fishing boats and 32 ft cutters (clinker built) for sailing. Among the fishing boats built there were *Romulas 1*, *Remus*, *Three Brothers II*, *Ern*. Types of timber used included oak, elm, pine, mahogany, larch and American whitewood. Early saws used were pitsaws and hand bandsaws, later with motors installed. Engines fitted on the various craft included Listers, Thorecroft and Kelvins, as used in whelk boats. Work was normally carried out for forty-eight hours a week (7–5; 1 o'clock Saturday). Boat builders pictured (*c.* 1946) from top left are: -?-, Taffy Mathews, -?-, Norman Kelsey, ? Webb, Roy ?, Bob West, ? Wood, Harry Fagg, Jack Sinclair, Ron Barton, Jack Wybourne, Don Dell, Eric Camburn, ? Rivers, George Pattenden, Sam Barton, George Pattenden sen., -?-, Sid Luckhurst, Jack Hunnisett, -?-, Ted Mayhew, Allen Dudley, Dick Perkins (cousin of R.J.). Sitting: Cally Croft, Roy Saddleton, Bubbles Hammond, ? Fisk, Jack Mayhew, Oggie Laker, Dido Foreman.

Safely harboured whelk boats nestle together on the east side, near the part known as 'Deadmans Corner', in 1937. In the distance, close to the mouth of the Harbour, moored against the east quay is the motor vessel *Actuosity* (400 tons) owned by Frank T. Everard & Sons. A long line of Andersons coal trucks is waiting to be loaded.

Two cargo vessels moored alongside the east quay of the Harbour in the early 1930s. The first one can be identified as the *Evelyn Manor* built at Fox Hol, Holland, in 1920, gross weight 396 tons, net 226, owned by John Allison of Dundee, later owners Dundee, Perth & London Shipping Co. She was engaged mainly with coastal work – coal, ballast, etc.

At the Pier Head, leaving Whitstable Harbour on 20 July 1935, is the cargo vessel *Noss Head*. One of many iron-hulled ships to trade these shores after the earlier wooden-hulled brigs, brigantines, barquentines, etc., she was built in 1921, weighed 400 tons, and was owned at one time by Alexander F. Henry & Magregor Ltd of Leith, Scotland.

A row of smacks, with men standing on the decks, near Andersons Yard, Island Wall, *c.* 1922. One has been identified as the *Twinns*, built in 1884, 33 ft long, weighing 10 tons, owned by Mr H.J. Paysden and broken up in 1930.

A barge, one of many that used to visit these shores, lies off the Horsebridge, *c.* 1930. Children play in the water around her, climb aboard her and sit on her deck. As the tide went out the horse and carts would arrive and provisions and materials would be unloaded onto them and taken ashore.

SECTION SIX

Entertainment, Sport and Leisure

A performance by the Whitstable Operatic Society at St Mary's Hall, Oxford Street in the 1920s. Here we see, from the left, Charlie Cook, Nell Fitkin and Tom Rigden in one of the many shows that were staged there. These included *Chinese Honeymoon*, *Earl and the Girl*, *Flora Dora*, and *The Dancing Mistress*. Performers included Mr Dunkin, Mrs Pettman, Mrs Rigden, Ken Amos, Les Hall, Bill Steed, Bill Skeats, Mr Wilman, Ida Rising and Madam Wainwright, who played a leading role as a singer. (She also had a baby linen shop in the town.) Performances, held on Tuesday, Wednesday, Thursday and Saturday nights, starting at 8 and finishing at 10.30, were well attended. Rehearsals were held at the Bear & Key on Friday evenings, dress rehearsals on Monday nights. Bookings for the shows could be obtained from Willmans Furniture Store, front seats 2s 6d, back seats 1s 6d. Shows continued until the Second World War.

Quite a versatile character on and off stage was Tom Rigden, pictured here in all whites with blackened face in one of his operatic performances at the Parish Hall in the 1920s. During the day he took deliveries and ran his own corn merchants shop, together with his wife Adelaide, at 23 High Street, right next to the Fire Station, where Tom was a volunteer fireman from 1912 to 1936 and drove the 'Old Native' engine. His father was Captain of the brigade for some of the time. As the family lived behind the station, when emergency calls were taken Tom would summon the other firemen by launching a maroon (rocket) from the back yard, where the old engine was kept. During this time he also helped run a garage, which his father had bought from Mr Breach in Oxford Street in the early '20s. Tom had an early French-built Delauny Bellville charabanc in which he would take people on all sorts of outings. The second charabanc he owned was an old Daimler. Later his father had a garage built at No. 14 Canterbury Road. Just before and during the last war Tom also drove an ambulance which was kept at the Horsebridge.

Members of the cast from the Whitstable Operatic Society on stage at the St Mary's Parish Hall, *c.* 1928. The cast includes, from the left, Mrs Rigden (sitting), her husband Tom (third left) and over to the right, sitting with the dog, Charlie Cook and Nell Fitkin.

This D. West photograph features a popular group of entertainers called the 'Lead Swingers' around the '20s. They used to perform at the Palais-de-Luxe cinema and concert hall in Harbour Street, which was opened just before the First World War.

Jimmy Woods and his Royal Sports Concert Party, Whitstable-on-Sea, pictured here for their 1916 season at what was known as the 'Pavilion', a small building which stood opposite the Tankerton Hotel on the top of the Slopes. Pictured from the left are Winnie Usher, Jimmy Wood, Ethel Langdon, Minnie Faulkner, Charlie Charlton, Dorothy Anderson and Cecil Downton.

Members of the Lawn Concert Party, on stage at the 'Pavilion', on the Slopes, Marine Parade, Tankerton, from a B.W. Fisk-Moore photograph of 1923. These shows provided popular entertainment for visitors and locals alike.

Some of the talented soldiers appearing on stage at the Argosy cinema, *c.* 1940, in a musical revue entitled *Thumbs-Up!*, in aid of the Troops Welfare Fund. Part 1 featured 'One between Two', with Ray Gibbs and Bill Anthony on piano; appearing in 'Dance of Desire' were Roy Pearce and Pat Hitchen; 2nd Lt Jenkins, who was responsible for the revue, can be seen with easel during his act 'The Big Drawer'.

THE ARGOSY, WHITSTABLE

THE MUSTARD-POTS

(DIVISION CONCERT PARTY)

PRESENT A

"Condimendable" Musical Revue

THUMBS-UP!

By kind permission of

Maj.-Gen. R. V. POLLOK, C.B., C.B.E., D.S.O.

WITH AN ALL TROOP CAST
DRAWN FROM THE DIVISION

IN AID OF THE TROOPS WELFARE FUND

THE "MUSTARD-POTS"

formed by and the Revue produced by 2/Lieut. M. B. Jenkins

Programme : Twopence

The programme front.

The front of the Argosy cinema in the High Street, illuminated with bunting and a crown to celebrate the coronation of King George VI in 1937. The cinema, which opened earlier that year, is showing *Dressed to Kill*, starring Clive Brook and Tutta Rolf. Admission was Circle 1s 6d and 1s 3d, Stalls 1s and 9d and 6d; children were half price. This later became the Regal cinema.

This comic postcard comes from the Dainty series, a long line of watercolour cards published by E.T.W. Dennis & Sons Ltd, and is the work of artist Biggar. Their earliest postcards were published in about 1901.

John Sanger & Sons' Circus at Whitstable. In the days before the First World War people, especially children, would get excited at the arrival of the circus, held on open ground between Cromwell Road and Regent Street, close to Hamilton Road. Here we see big cats (lions in fact) inside a cage mounted on a trailer. Once the main tent had been erected, the circus would often set off for the High Street, parading most of the animals, including elephants, camels, giraffes, buffaloes, and rhinoceroses. With two performances a day, they stayed for a week. Another circus that came to town was Fossett's.

The 1933 Whitstable Carnival assembles outside W. Hayward's coach builders, Cromwell Road. The Sea Cadet unit's clown 'Ello', alias PO S. Wraight, and his 'horse' amuse the crowd.

Residents and shopkeepers of Tankerton Circus joined together to organize a carnival float in 1929. Dressed in costumes for the occasion, among the people included are Mr and Mrs Emmerson (shopkeepers), Councillor Watts (wine shop), D. Wild (solicitor) and Mrs Thompson. All are pictured in Cromwell Road.

The Whitstable Wesleyan FC 1909–10, outside the old school next to the chapel in Argyle Road. They usually played at the 'Salts', West Cliff. The team includes, from top left, Danny Sharp, Harry Saddleton and Charlie Porter, who later became a builder in the town.

This group of football players was photographed on Good Friday 1921 by the old Drill Hall next to the 'rec' ground. The team pictured is, standing, left to right: Billy Barham, Buster Snelling (goalkeeper), who went on the play for the town, and Herbert Blythe. Kneeling are Horace Carden (right half-back), Jack Hudson (centre half) and Charlie Allen (left half-back). Front row: ? Pullen (outside right), Alan Hawkins (inside right) Bill Bright (centre forward), Charlie Botting (inside left), and Jimmy Gann.

The Whitstable cricket team of 1908, pictured together at the Manor House ground in Alexandra Road. Although cricket was first played at Belmont in the mid-1870s this ground was also used at times. Those pictured include, back row: 3rd from left Roy Cox, 5th Mr Dilnot, 6th C. Rowden, 8th Dr Etheridge. Front row, 3rd from left J. Powell, 4th H. Ashby, 6th A. Harrison.

The Whitstable horse shows were held on the Belmont ground. These shows, which dated to the early '20s, were a popular event. Among the prizes were a rose bowl and, for the best lady rider, the *Whitstable Times* riding crop.

Whitstable Cycling Club members out on a run at Ramsgate seafront in 1938. Those pictured are, from the left: Henry Frend, Squib Whorlow, Dennis Churcher, Ken Bourne, -?-, -?-, -?-, Horace Laraman, Geoff Hayward, Alf Revell, ? Binns. The club was established in 1935 in a beach hut at West Beach, moved later to premises behind Webbs paper shop, High Street, from there to a large wooden hut in Beresford Road where they had recreational facilities, and eventually to a brick building, which later became Bartons yacht fittings. Cycle runs were planned from these buildings for most weekends. Ten to twenty members would usually participate. A favourite short run was to 'Penny Pot' near Chartham, where the pub had an inviting open fire and used oil lamps. Tea with as much as you could eat cost just one shilling. Other runs were to Woodchurch, Stouting, Doddington, Broadstairs, Hythe, Ash, Dover, Lenham. One Easter they went to Herne Hill (London), where a heavy snow storm was encountered. On a trip to Hastings the members had to sleep on the beach, arriving too late to find B&B accommodation. The club fizzled out after the war.

Looking along Beach Walk at the modernistic façade of the well-known Jacques amusement arcade. This was a popular haunt not only for visitors in the '50s and '60s, but for locals as well, who would congregate there especially to listen to the juke-box blaring out the hits of the time. As well as the different types of machines, you could play bingo or just sit and eat the freshly caught seafood. Mr Archie Watts was the proprietor after Jacques, but Fred Butcher was the familiar figure: he could often be seen with dozens of keys strung around his neck. He must have had a lot of patience!

This early arcade could be found along Beach Walk in the mid-'20s. Among the fruit machines on the left is a Kalloscope which reads 'put a penny in the slot to see a series of beautiful pictures' (semi-nude women). Those pictured include, third from right (the boy), Norman Fuggle and, second from right, Alf Foreman.

Not quite Aviemore, but Whitstable's own ski resort nevertheless. High up on Duncan Downs people can be seen enjoying themselves tobogganing, while in the distance, over the town as far as the eye can see, the rooftops are all the same colour! This picture was taken around 1938.

The roller-skating rink situated between Sea Wall and Sea Street was a popular venue in the early years, having opened in 1914. This picture looks towards Sea Wall and Reeves Beach, *c.* 1915. The building at the side was the rink café, with, underneath, the changing rooms. Occasionally you could skate to music played on the organ. Children would get there as early as 7.30 on a Saturday morning and for an hour or more, with no music playing and with their own skates, it would cost 6d (half price). With skates provided it was 1s 6d. There were also competitions for dancing.

Many people must remember the boating lake, situated at the end of West Beach and to the side of the golf course, with great affection. Families would enjoy themselves here, rowing and canoeing for a few pennies. This picture was taken in the '50s before the boating lake eventually closed in the '70s and was later filled in.

Above the beach at Tankerton, just off Tower Hill, where one could sit out in pleasant surroundings and enjoy drinks or use the putting green. In the 1700s copperas were collected from the beach in this area, having been washed from the surrounding earth. It was used to produce sulphate of iron and iron pyrites.

Yachting at Whitstable before the First World War. These large single-masted yachts, with huge main sails and clipper-shaped bows, look very graceful cutting through the water. They were probably individually built at local boatyards. The top picture shows a yacht off Long Beach, close to the Harbour; below are several yachts off Tankerton.

SECTION SEVEN

People and Events

The man himself – Dan Sherrin, artist, woodcarver, businessman, practical joker, sportsman, fundraiser and local personality, draws a crowd at the Horsebridge, outside Brownings coal yard, during one of his visits there in the '20s. Pictured high up on his Seasalter Fire Brigade tender, he was no doubt arousing the people's interest.

It's that man again – playing the clown in this photograph taken at Belmont playing fields by Mr S. West, *c.* 1930. Note the clothing: square-patterned plus-four tweed suit with (very loud) matching hat and white ankle gaiters. What can one say about this man that's not been said before?

This group of soldiers from the Kent Cyclists' Regiment, pictured at the old Coast Guard Station, West Beach, is from a Fisk-Moore postcard dated 14 October 1915. The Old Neptune public house can be seen in the background. The back of this card, sent by one of the soldiers, reads, 'I don't know yet what I am doing, think I am going munition making, shall let you know later, this is our lot at Whitstable lookout station, here for a fortnight.'

Local soldiers and sailors, *c.* 1915. Standing, left to right: 'Yiddy' Pidduck (blacksmith), Bill Bennett (builder), Soup Coleman (?), Bert Bennett (builder). Front row: ? Skinner, George Pattenden (shipyard), ? Appleton, ? Gambrill.

Old Mr Norris of Surman's, the butchers in the High Street, can be seen here at the back of the shop getting a few chickens ready for sale in the 1930s. He was in charge of the butchery side.

Henry George Surman, local butcher, and his wife, Ellen Harriet, pictured behind their shop at 59–61 High Street, *c.* 1914. The children, all boys, are, from the left, Percy, who went on to be a headmaster at Rochester, George, at the back, later a butcher, Sidney, in front, later also a butcher, and, to the right, Bert, who became a headteacher in the West Country. Only Sidney survives today.

Fishmonger Mr Robert Court and his wife Eliza, standing near their shop at 66 Oxford Street, which they had for almost thirty years, *c.* 1914. Before that it had been a florists.

Mr A.G. Humphrey stands at the doorway of his home at 34 Albert Street, where he worked as a watchmaker and jeweller. A sign advertises the fact. This picture was taken in 1926.

Captain George Fisher, of Whitstable Volunteer Fire Brigade, 1930s. He worked at Andersons Shipyard as a blacksmith and lived in Nelson Road. In the First World War he was an Army sergeant. This portrait was taken by B. Reeves.

Wartime Tankerton. The Auxiliary Fire Service are pictured outside George Fitt Motors, where they were billeted in an office from 1940 to 1941. In the back row are Sid Hatchard and ? Newman; in front are Ben Webb, Punch Olive and Len Rigden. Their next duty was at the Old Troc cinema until 1945. Other billets were at the Horsebridge, the corner of Church Street, Bartletts Corner and the bottom of Borstal Hill.

The pupils pictured here are from the Soderberg Private School in Nelson Road. Mrs Effie Soderberg on the left ran the small school for some years; prior to this she was in charge of the juniors at the Board School. The lady on the right is unknown; back row, second from right is Ron Foad. The school ran from 1934 until the '40s. This photograph was taken in the '30s.

Whitstable Baptists outside the church in Middle Wall, *c.* 1930. Back row, left to right: Bown, Andrews (builder), Staddon (watchmaker), King (policeman), Hayatt. Front row: Brett (florist), Mann, Revd S.C. Harrison, Fullick, Collar (shipwright).

This picture shows the late Douglas West – the photographer responsible for many of the fine photographs of Whitstable and its people over many years – in action. This occasion was the handing over of the Ceremonial Mace, in memory of Mrs Min Camburn, at St Alphege church, *c.* 1960. Second from right is Douglas West with his Minolta camera. The others, from the left, are Ted Camburn, Lt Charlie Camburn, and Drum Major Gaskin.

The adult 'Vigilant' life-saving team. The squad was formed by Lt Charles Camburn in the early '30s and this picture was taken in September 1934. The members pictured include, back row centre, George Nye, second from right, C. Poole, far right, George Taylor. Front row: ? Shrubshall, Lt C. Camburn, A. Weller (instructor), Alan Stroud and, sitting with the sign, Jim Wallace.

The Whitstable Sea Cadets grouped together along Cromwell Road beside their carnival float, *c.* 1930. Officer Lt Charlie Camburn (Mr Sea Cadet himself) is standing far left. The theme of the float was the forthcoming Chatham Navy Week. The unit, the oldest in the country, was originally known as the Wesleyan Sunday School Fife & Drum Band and was first formed in 1854.

Members of the Whitstable Sea Cadets in the High Street alongside their barrel organ while collecting for Flag Day, *c.* 1950. Members include Harry Crooks, -?-, Charlie Camburn, ? Gilham, Philip Sheperd, Bob Nutten and Bill (Cod) Kelsey.

The four Eastern ladies known as the 'Giraffe Neck Women', so named because of the rings which stretched their necks. This picture was taken inside the Duke of Cumberland Hotel around 1934 by Mr S. West. The women arrived by stage coach from a circus visiting Canterbury. A notice behind the bar indicates that the women were to be there on Thursday 10 September to sample the Whitstable native oysters. Mr Frosty Hatton can be seen serving the oysters; just to his right in the crowd is Beryl Waters, whose father ran the Pearsons Arms; behind the bar is Jack Robinson, and next to him is his sister Mrs Smith, landlady of the Duke of Cumberland at the time.

Beryl Waters prepares to pull a pint for the photographer in the Pearsons Arms at the Horsebridge in the '50s. A popular landlady for many years, Beryl practically grew up here, having taken over from her father Charles, the previous landlord of this Whitbread pub. Many of her customers were from the 'seafaring fraternity'. Note the lovely old willow patterned porcelain handles which were a feature for many years. The pub dates back to the 1850s.

A group pictured outside the Royal Sovereign public house in Victoria Street, *c.* 1934. An East Kent bus has been especially hired for the many regulars, often local tradesmen, who attended this annual event. Among the people identified are, seated second left, Bill Rigden, Jack Cage, and Laurie Beadle (landlord). At the back, tenth from left, is Bill Terry; next to him is ? Dunn.

Trying to give this horse some advice at Radfall Riding Stables is World Champion boxer Freddie Mills during a visit to Whitstable on 26 February 1949. With him is jockey Brian Lee Alliston. Freddie was a friend of his family's for many years. He learnt boxing the hard way – in the fairground booths. In June 1942 in London he won the British & Empire Light Heavyweight titles by knocking out veteran Len Harvey inside two rounds. In 1944 he fought Jack London in Manchester for the Heavyweight Championship of Great Britain, losing on points over fifteen rounds. In May 1946 Gus Lesnevich, the Light Heavyweight Champion of the World, fought Freddie in Harringay, but Lesnevich held the title after the referee stopped the fight in the tenth round. In the rematch in 1948 Freddie won the title on points from Lesnevich over fifteen rounds at White City. In January 1950, at Earls Court, Freddie lost his world title to Joe Maxim in round 10 by a knockout and announced his retirement soon afterwards.

Local people will remember Burt Silk, an old fashioned character who delivered milk collected from the Manor Farm Dairy, Church Street from a horse and cart in the South Street–Chestfield–Radfall areas between the '30s and '50s. He is pictured here outside his home on land opposite the South Street–Radfall Corner junction in 1952. With his wife Rose, who was equally old fashioned, he kept goats and chickens. In the evenings one would find Burt out the back in a huge wooden shed, with oil lamp burning, repairing bicycles. There were frames, wheels, saddles, and parts hanging on bits of string everywhere and a long work bench was crammed with old tools. My first bicycle was purchased from him. When delivering milk in the rain it wasn't unusual for Burt to wear several raincoats and as many trilby hats. Nor would the snow deter him. He would deliver part of his round using a large sledge, which he pulled himself. Sometimes his horse Dolly moved off on her own and Burt would be seen chasing after her shouting 'Get Back!' As children, at weekends we would meet the cart at the top of the hill, where Burt was ready for his last run, and he would shout 'Hold on tight' as we all jumped aboard, clinging to each other as he galloped off, rapidly gathering speed. What a thrill! Burt died in 1958.

Baptists and other Sunday schools congregate together in 1903 to march down the High Street, some carrying banners. The occasion was a rally with a picnic later. Joining them are the Sea Cadet Fife & Drum Band. This unit, the oldest in the country, was formed in 1854; after 1904 it became the Drum & Bugle Band.

These men in naval uniform are outside Customs House, No. 4 Gladstone Road, where the call up for the Royal Naval Reserve was held for local people, in 1914. Among those pictured here are Jim Rowden and ? Stroud, two men who survived when HMS *Cressy* went down in the early part of the war.

Whitstable mourns King Edward VII on 20 May 1910. A crowd gathers outside St Alphege church in the High Street. The building in the centre of the picture is the Queens Head Inn.

An old horse-drawn fire tender passes up the High Street, for the funeral of a fireman killed on duty, while colleagues march alongside, *c.* 1914. Leading the procession is Mr Fred Porter.

The back of this photograph of the 1st Whitstable Scout Band reads, '14th July 1924, Band contest'. I believe it was taken in the Dane John Gardens in Canterbury. Back row, left to right: Ernie Austin, T. Court, H. Hope, Les Hall, Chas Farrow, George Ford. Centre row: Dick Rigden, F. Thundow, J. Neame, J. Bright, -?- (with flag). Front row: ? Hollibon, ? Farrow, Rupert Fox, W. Newman, Warwick Wright, Bill Blyth (who started the band in 1919), Charlie Blyth, Tom Rigden, Doody Blyth, Sam Blyth. On the ground: S. Marais, H. Thundow.

August 1933 Carnival. The Whitstable Scout Band followed by the Whitstable Firemen on the 'Old Native' engine, photographed from above D. West's High Street shop. Note the people standing on the window ledge of Barclays Bank.

Whitstable Salvation Army Band at Tower Hill, Tankerton on King George V Jubilee Day 1935. Left to right: Bob Cox, Chris Cox, Bob Able, Cecil Carter, Gordon Blyth, Jim Davis, George Blackman, -?-, -?-, Charlie Blyth, -?-, Les Kendall, Bill Coveney, Bill Griggs. The band is one of the oldest in the town.

Early carnivals were among the big events of the year, and a lot of work went into preparing the various floats. In this picture, taken by West & Son *c.* 1926, at the gathering of the procession in the Cromwell Road area, and showing old prams of the day complete with adverts, the 'babies' seem contented.

In this carnival picture of around 1926, taken at the junction of Cromwell Road and Railway Avenue, a pram is being used as a large collection box requesting pennies for the PDSA (People's Dispensary for Sick Animals).

Fireman's wedding at Whitstable between Mr H.B. Blyth and the late Miss Marjorie Olive Beer at All Saints' church, 1929. The bridegroom – 'Doody', as he was known – was taken to church on the fire engine, which caused some excitement. The Revd G. Hillyard officiated. On leaving, the bride and groom passed under archways of axes held by firemen and staves held by the 1st Whitstable Scouts. This shows father of the groom, Mr William Blyth, in Scout uniform, with members of the brigade on board the Old Merryweather fire engine in Church Street. Tom Rigden is at the wheel, getting ready to tow the wedding car away.

An old steam train awaits, a crowd gathers to bid farewell, a British Rail official stands at the front – the occasion is the last train to leave Whitstable for Canterbury on the 'Crab & Winkle' line, in November 1952. The line was closed only to be reopened again in February 1953, when the main line between Whitstable and Faversham was flooded. The lower photograph shows the tail end of the last train as it disappears past the second station on the other side of the crossing. Once the main line had been fixed, the old line, in use since 1830, closed for good.

SECTION EIGHT

Out and About

The Beer Outing from the Bear Inn, Faversham. This postcard photograph was taken by local photographer T.U. Barber in 1924. The men, all wearing hats and buttonholes, are gathered together in Court Street just before their journey. Whitstable's Tom Rigden, wearing the white coat, stands by his old Daimler charabanc and with him at his side is his son Len. Faversham's old charabanc is on the other side. The outing, which started at 8 a.m. on a Sunday in June, took them to Canterbury, Ashford, Bethersden, Biddenden, Tenterden, Northiam, Rye, New Romney, Dymchurch, Hythe, Elham Valley then home.

Hopping in Kent at a farm at Dargate during the last war. Pictured left to right are Richard Chapman, his mother Freda, her mother Caroline Nicholls, Aunt Sue and Aunt Annie Keen. They travelled to the fields on a bus, leaving from outside the Noah's Ark public house at around 6 a.m. and not returning until 6 or 7 in the evening. Work was spread over six days a week. Extra was paid for working during the war years. In order to earn a good living, the whole family often worked together and even the children would help, the 'tallyman' occasionally finding one at the bottom of a Londoner's bin!

This wooden bungalow, situated off the Pilgrims Lane, was the one-time home of Charlie Knowles, fruiterer. However, the property, pictured here in the '30s, was soon to come down. Mr Knowles purchased the land and obtained the timber for the bungalows in the early '20s from a Wembley Empire Exhibition. (The bungalows were later named 1 and 2 Wembley Villas.) Charlie had the buildings erected thinking there would not be a problem, but the council thought otherwise and condemned them for having no planning permission. Incensed with this decision, Charlie started a campaign to keep his home. This postcard was used to gain publicity, and printed on the back was a letter asking for 'British Justice'. On one occasion Charlie went along to the council offices at the Castle with his son Gordon who was holding a placard, to be revealed on his father's nod, which read, 'Father forgive them for they know not what they do'. He even locked the council officials in the Castle and had 'Oh my poor Bungalow' printed on his fruit boxes. But these things were to no avail. The bungalow, now rented by his employee, Mr J. Willis, who was given until Christmas Day 1937 to vacate, was demolished, Mr Knowles bearing the cost.

Open fields and a few tents: the early beginnings of the Alberta Caravan Park, when it was known as a camping ground, at Seasalter, *c*. 1935. The name reportedly derives from a Canadian who came over, leased the land, and called it 'Alberta'.

The Blue Anchor pub, Seasalter, an old established house dating back to the 1600s, which was frequented by many a camper from the Alberta Camp Site opposite. To the left is the fruit and veg stall that was there in the '50s and '60s.

On a cold and windy day at Seasalter a group gathers for the ceremony of Extending the Parish Boundaries, *c.* 1938. Among those attending are, second from the right, Councillor Fred Watts, Tommy Stow (clerk), Town Beadle Lou Turner, Chairman Jim Wood, holding the scroll, Councillor John Pragnell, Archie Baker (clerk), Councillor Cecil Edkins and, sixth from left, Geoff Marsh (a weights clerk).

Nurses surrounded by soldiers from, among others, the Buffs Artillery and Scotch regiments, some wounded, gathered outside the old Seasalter Battery on the seafront. The wooden buildings were used during that period as billets and an MOD convalescent home. The nurse second from left in the top row has been identified as Dot Carson. This is a black and white Fisk-Moore postcard of around 1916.

Relaxing in the sunshine outside the Seasalter Post Office and Stores, the minerals on the tables having been bought from the little stall at the side of the stores, in a photograph taken around 1939. The owner at the time was a P. Hughes. Today the property is still a stores and post office.

'Tree Tops' Guest House, Joy Lane, rebuilt after a fire almost destroyed it in the late '20s when it was a private bungalow named Rosary.

Looking down a quiet Joy Lane towards Whitstable, showing the old Rose in Bloom pub as it was in the 1940s. The pub was established in 1894, with E.A. Hunt as its first landlady. Local artist Dan Sherrin lived behind the trees next door at 'Westbank'.

Seasalter golf links, *c.* 1919. This family dressed in their Sunday outfits are standing across the dyke on a plank, which seems to be bowing! West Cliff can clearly be seen over to one side. The golf course was established around 1911 with 9 holes and probably one of the lowest fairway levels around.

Looking down from Borstal Hill, *c.* 1913. In the distance, sitting high up on a slipway, a barquentine with its tall masts dominates the shoreline along West Beach.

The windmill off Borstall Hill, *c.* 1913. In this early view the area looks very open but over the years it has been built over. The windmill, built around 1806, was a focal point for ships, etc.

Church Street, *c.* 1909, looking up towards the Old Forge on the right. A Mr Hodges was the blacksmith at the time. Opposite stands The Monument public house. The Oxford Street Bakery delivery cart can be seen passing by on its round. This particular area, one of the oldest parts of the town, was traditionally regarded as a village.

Pictured at Orchard Close, Tankerton in the mid-'30s, his small hand-cart loaded with ladders and other materials, is Mr F.D. Chalmers. The cart reads, 'Painter, Decorator, Window Cleaner, Odd Jobs Done.'

Milk ladies Queenie (on the left) and Ivy Revel, at Kingsdown Park, Tankerton during the last war, when the men were away. As early as 6 a.m. they collected the milk from Bartletts Dairy, at the corner of Church Street, and set out for Tankerton, pushing their large three-wheeled cart. They arrived back at 2 p.m. and worked seven days a week for the sum of £6 between them. During the winter customers would offer them tea, but they would also stop to buy cakes from Turners at 103 Tankerton Road. Queenie also delivered newspapers first thing in the morning for Luckhursts for 5s. a week. On some afternoons they biked out to Bartletts fields, to hoe the 'worzels', and occasional evenings were spent bottling up in the dairy.

Mrs Morris is greeted with a bouquet of flowers by Maud Rigden, the occasion being the cutting of the first turf for the building of the Whitstable and Tankerton Hospital in September 1925. In October 1925 the foundation stone was laid by Lord Northbourne and the hospital was opened in December 1926 by Colonel Carnegie CBE.

The Whitstable and Tankerton Cottage and Convalescent Hospital, 1940. Opened in 1926, it was supported by voluntary contributions. This postcard was sent by a nurse at the hospital to her mum and dad, and some of the message reads, 'I will ask the matron about getting me off half an hour early. I am sure she will oblige, seeing she likes me so much.'

Northwood Road, Tankerton, showing York House, the grocery and confectionery shop, on the corner of Pier Avenue, opposite Tankerton Hospital, *c.* 1936. Established in 1925, the shop was owned by L. Needham.

A man on a motorbike passes along a quiet Herne Bay Road, Swalecliffe, *c.* 1920. On the left is an old thatched cottage, at one time the post office, and on the right, close to the roadside, is the original Wheatsheaf public house, est. 1851.

Children ready to celebrate May Day, *c.* 1914, outside the old Swalecliffe Preparatory School. They are dressed in white with flower garlands and head-dresses. Seated on her pony and trap behind is the May Queen.

A group of parents, sisters and brothers having tea during a visit to the Scouts camp, in a lovely early photograph taken near the original Coastguard Station, Swalecliffe, on 23 September 1911, by W. Hargreaves.

Kite Farm Camps Ltd, otherwise known as Seaview Camp Site, Swalecliffe, 1938. One of the larger camps, it was started on land owned by the Pout family in the '20s.

Children play near the flag-pole outside the Victorian-built cottages which became the Swalecliffe Coastguard Station, housing one officer, his men and their families, in 1912. This was located near Seaview Holiday Camp.

CHESTFIELD-ON-SEA KENT.

Between CANTERBURY, HERNE BAY & WHITSTABLE.

Main Line CHESTFIELD STATION now OPEN.

UNSPOILED COUNTRYSIDE.

CHESTFIELD GOLF COURSE
(SHRUB HILL)
-mile from Station.

'PHONES:
Chestfield 33.
" 12.

THE OLD BARN TEA-ROOMS

Country Houses Cottages and Sites
in this
LOVELY OLD VILLAGE.

APPLY:—*RESIDENT OWNER,*
GEORGE REEVES, Chestfield Village, Nr. Whitstable, Kent.

An advert from the 1920s promoting Chestfield as the ideal place to live at the time, with lots of open spaces and quite peaceful. It was published for the Reeves Dynasty, who owned a considerable amount of the area including the golf course.

The view from above Chestfield village in around 1928, showing the Oast Houses, Old Barn Golf Club and Old Farm House (top right). Some of the fairways can also be seen. The picture was taken by Tom Wesson in a Dessoutter and developed by West & Son.

Part of the Old Balsar Farm, Chestfield in 1935. The round thatched building to the right was once a store, then an office, and was later used partly for a bus shelter. Behind stands the large fourteenth-century Tythe Barn, at one time the club house, then tea rooms and, recently, a restaurant. Beyond that is one of the first oast-houses to be converted to a private residence in the area.

The interior of the old Tythe Barn, Chestfield, complete with huge inglenook and original beams. A golf clubhouse in the '20s, it later became tea rooms. In the '50s the building had an atmosphere all of its own. There were all types of relics and artefacts to be seen, including armour, shields, spears and swords hanging from the walls.

Young ladies relax in their best dresses and bonnets in the long meadow grass, as families on a church outing congregate at Chestfield in 1910.

Some of the men who worked for George Reeves, the builders, at Chestfield in the '20s. Mr Reeves developed the area at the time, most homes being constructed of Tudor design. This group includes, far left, B. Foreman (carpenter), next Fred Page or 'Trunky' (bricklayer), fourth Bunny Piddock, then Bill Coveney.

Harvesting in the fields of Whitstable on the 'Gilberts', Millstrood Farm, *c.* 1922. Three strong horses are hard at work pulling along an old harvesting machine. Mr Alfred Gilbert took on the farm in 1919 and ran it until the mid-'50s. Apart from arable land, he had cattle, pigs, chickens and turkeys on the 200 acre farm, and lived at Golden Hill. The man holding the sheaf of corn and wearing a top hat is Mr Harry Wheeler, a relation of Mr Gilbert. In his younger days Harry was a fisherman.

High snow drifts at the top of Red Bridge Hill, near Radfall, in January 1940. These council workmen are digging their way along the road in order to make it passable.

A familiar site in the woods at Radfall in the '50s was the charcoal burner with his blackened face, tending the fire under his huge round metal drums which were normally filled with silver birch and covered over. A small chimney was let into the side of the drum, and smoke rose gently into the air. One use for the charcoal was in the process of making gunpowder.

Homeward-bound baker Mr Fred Hawkins and son Frank on the way to South Street, at the bottom of Red Bridge Hill near the 'Brook' Stream, after delivering to Herne Bay, Herne Street and Chestfield. Their outward journey, which started in the morning and was done three times a week, would take them to Tankerton, Swalecliffe and Herne Bay, and back via South Street, sometimes arriving home at 7 o'clock in the evening. The horse and cart were kept at stables in Middle Wall next to the Congregational Hall.

Crossways Farm, Radfall, 1928. Brothers Burt, John and Ernie Silk worked the arable land between Chestfield Road and Radfall Corner. Ernie leans against the large open wagon, while holding the horse is Fred Collar.

Local man Burt Silk, a keen horseman, is pictured dressed in his best suit on the farm at Radfall with a Welsh pony, *c.* 1920. When visiting the town he would often ride, tying his horse up at the stables behind the Bear & Key. (See p. 129.)

Radfall corner shop, with proprietor and family, *c.* 1930. Pictured from the right are shopkeeper Ernest Silk, wife Isobel, sons Sibert and Ernie, Mrs Rose Silk (sister-in-law) and Ernest's third son Harry.

Pictured in 1954 with horse and cart belonging to brother-in-law Burt, the local milkman, is Mrs Isobel Silk outside the shop she ran for many years after the death of her husband Ernest (Jumbo). The shop was the focal point for the small hamlet of Radfall. I used to look forward to Saturdays, when I would go down to the shop and spend 6d on sweets. Mrs Silk carried on running the business into her eighties, eventually closing in 1968. She died a year later.

Acknowledgements

I would like to thank the following people for their interest, help and kind cooperation during my research in compiling this book.

Mr and Mrs F.W. Ackling • Mr Lionel Browning • Mrs Shirley Browning Mrs M. Bowman • Mr H. Butcher • Mr Derek Butler • Mrs J. Camburn Canterbury and East Kent Postcard Club Library • Ernie Castle Freda Chapman • Harold Coleman • Alan Coles • Mrs Emerson • Alf Ericson Brian Hadler • Mrs K. Halls • Anne Hammond • Wallace Harvey Alan Hawkins • Mr and Mrs Reg Hayward • Geoff Hayward • Mrs High Fred Hinkley • Laurence Horseman • Mr Keenan • Alf and Joan Leggatt Queenie Luckhurst • Norman Maflin • Mrs M.L. Martin • Marjorie Merritt George Pattenden • Len Rigden • Mrs M. Rigden • Jack Sharp • George Silk Ms N.R. Silk • Steve Silk • Joan Smith • Mrs G.L. Surman Mr Sydney Surman • Douglas West • Mrs Wheeler and those I may have overlooked.

I regret that due to lack of space on some pages I have had to condense the information and reminiscences.

Finally, my thanks go to my wife, Linda, for undertaking the typing of the manuscripts and providing the coffee and biscuits, and also to my children, Teresa, Tracey and Aaron, for providing the headache pills!